Joe Maxime

Impressum

Joe Maxime

Copyright © 2023 Joe Maxime

Alle Rechte vorbehalten.

Die Coverseite wurde auf canva.com erstellt.

HOW TO LIVE LIFE

How am I supposed to know who I am if I do not try out a lot

How should I know if psychology is the right subject to study

Or sport science in a master degree

How should I know without trying

With trying there are errors

There are failures

But only if you fail enough times you are ready to succeed

You can only have a clue what you like, if you try in what you are good at, what you love spending your time with

Just try out a lot of stuff out

How can you can fully certain if you have not tried it

With a fully open mind

How am I supposed to know if I did not try it

Believing everything you think you know about yourself

Why are you trying to explain why you are not that kind of person

Why not try it out

And then begin to judge

Can you please just stop to explain how and why you
become that person

Who you think you are today?

Who you become

You are not a museum

You don´t have to show you past to everyone

Maybe just don´t take your past that seriously

Just be open minded

And try things

If you fail

Or get hurt

That´s life

But what if you succeed

That is life too

If you are happy

You gained so much

Hopefully you will fail a lot

So you know when you are really happy

HEALING YOURSELF BY HEALING OTHERS

I am healing myself

By helping others

By being the non-biological big sister for my best friend

It is kind of like being or becoming my own big sister

Reliving a situation

Where I ask for help

Where I begged my sister for help

And she did not give it to me at this moment

Because she was too weak

Maybe she still is

I found strength to build myself a life

Where I can give the person

Who is in the exact same spot as I was

The thing I was asking for

I became my own big sister

Also the big sister for my best friend

By giving her stuff I wanted to have but never gotten

Reliving, rethinking and regaining new experiences

Healing myself from that

I become the person I needed the most

I am proud of that

I am healing myself through this

WOMEN BECOMING MORE MASCULINE

Especially when their dad was emotionally absence in
their childhood

Do you know why you want kids?

Because you want to create life

That is feminine energy

But because you are acting so much time in your
masculine energy

you can´t love yourself

you want children because your kids will love you
unconditionally - no matter what

that is something I was looking out for my entire
life

I never got unconditional love

that is the real why I want children

#mindshiftingthought

RELATIONSHIP WITH YOURSELF

It is so much easier to dig yourself up
In somebody else's life and their problems
So deep
That you don't have to look at your own life
Filled with your own problems

You only gonna face their problems for them
Maybe you are helping them
Only because you know you can
But you get nothing in return
You get no help back
Not good for your trust issues

You had the hope
If you helped the other person enough
So the person is healed
Maybe the person will help you in return

Just people helping each other out
You help them
But the favor is not returned

You are standing there again

Hurt as fuck

You feeling too much again
You don´t know anymore anything
Everything you thought you know is falling apart

What if you built up a codependence
Again?
You put so much of your energy, work effort in this
So now you feel less
Again!

You feel tired all the time
You are not dealing with your stuff

Even if stuff from your past is coming up
You deal with her stuff first
Because you think
Her stuff is more important
Or you know you can help
Maybe she is worthier

Whatever

You are stepping back

You should start again

To follow the dopamine

Go where you have to go

Even if it hurts

But in the long run

It will be worth it

From now on

You have to become

More egocentric

You should stop to wait for anybody

You should not plan your life in dependency of somebody else's life plans

You are living your life waiting for others to help you

What is it you are hoping to get?

What are you expecting?

What is it only other persons could give you?

Love?

You can love yourself

Trust?

You can trust yourself more than anyone on this planet

Maybe this is where we should start together

We gotta start and learn to trust yourself first again

Start having faith in yourself

Trust yourself

Make yourself for yourself the most trustworthy person on this planet

So you will put yourself first - in every upcoming situation

Under every circumstances

You first

Me first

Even on a plane

You have to survive first to be able to help others

You need to have oxygen

Air to breathe

Don´t take your own air away

You have to trust yourself so you can rely on yourself anytime

In any crisis

You should become your best friend

You should at first have the healthiest relationship with yourself

Build your foundation

That is a lot of work

Because you are avoiding it so badly

You should do this now

Start now

.

Take yourself first

Try to teach yourself to trust yourself - again

It all starts with you

You should not be avoiding

Who you are

Who you trust

Trust yourself first

Be egocentric

So start following the dopamine

Take yourself first

Plan your life according to you

Don't let others slow you down

Fuck the others

Fuck the rest

Just do you

SHARING AND CARING

What is happiness

What is success worth?

If you Can't share it?

CONSISTENCY

I need someone consistent

Someone who says he will need 10 minutes

Will only take 10 minutes

Take this time He did say He would need

Or even better

Be faster

HEARTBROKEN

If my kid would treat me like that

I would be heartbroken

But the fact I don´t know

If my mom is

It does break my heart even more

PROUD OF ME

I am complete and complicated

I accept this now

#newproudme

LONG TERM GOAL

The long term goal is not to date them

It is to let them work for you

Because you have worked on yourself and your education

RE-OPEN WOUNDS

Living with you is not always fun

My childhood wounds getting triggered and ripped open

You trigger me in every way possible

But maybe for greater goods

I am becoming my best version

Healing my old and now again bleeding scars/wounds

TOXIC FAMILY SYSTEM

"Normal family"

To function while being angry at each other

While hating the other person – but still keep doing it for the other person

But only so the other person won´t know how deeply hurt you are

And still asking myself – how the other person can´t see the war fought in my head

Just Toxic

WISE WORDS - AFFIRMATION

Not my life

Not my choice

#Passi

HEALING STORY

Don't know what or who to trust

My feelings

My body is shivering

More and more trauma waking up inside of me

Letting my body shiver

Letting more trauma get to the surface

My body reacting to it -telling me to slow down? To process it all?

Am I doing something wrong?

Am I healing though?

By getting triggered more often

Realizing this

All those emotions crawling up my throat

Feeling like no air will fit through

Feels like suffocating

All too much

My body reacting with this overstimulation

By shivering

And me

At least I am shivering?

At least I let my body so much control

So he can shiver

I allow him to shiver?

So it can show me something is wrong

I don´t suppress it anymore

Is this a good sign?

My body showing me he is in distress?

Letting it all out?

Feeling everything

Hearing what my body has to tell me?

Is this healing?

Or is this again myself – sabotaging stage?

I am confused

What is right – what is wrong?

Is there such thing as right?

Is there – when it comes to healing?

Call me crazy

I think my body reacting

Shivering is a good sign

Me letting those feelings through

Telling myself it is okay to feel overwhelmed

It is okay to feel weak and all those nasty other
negative thoughts and affirmations my brain is
throwing at me – like old and greasy tomatoes

Which were (im)planted in my head

While I was little

These negative affirmations planted in my head

By the people who were supposed to love me (the most)

Telling myself no matter what

Because I will walk out of the dark

Even if I have to do it alone by myself

I am willing to learn to see (the) light

To become light

Which will lead me out of this darkness

By darkness I mean - my mind - dark black - poisoned by my toxic family

I am allowed to feel my body shivering

Maybe it is just my inner beast burning inside me

Awakening

Saying this is enough

Long enough it was sleeping

It is like Snow White

I am my own prince

And I decide now to willingly kiss my snow white

My trauma

Which was considered dead

I now kissed my Snow White

It is awake now

Healing can begin now

Because I – my own prince started the process

I will fight

I will now feel everything

I will never be dead inside again

I will never push away my feelings

Because the moment is not pleasant or right enough

I will never be in situations again

Where it is easier to leave my body and getting little parts of me killed in my own emotional and physical absence

I will never again – descendant from my own body -my own home

Never again

I am here on this earth to feel

Not to leave my body

Because not feeling a thing did not get me anywhere close I was planning to go

So this awakening won´t be easy – it will be awful to feel all those pushed away feelings

It will be exhausting but I will get through this with every shiver of my body

I know I am feeling more and more everyday

Maybe I will come to feeling everything one day

I know I am feeling everything I need to feel at this moment

It will be my healing story

SITUATION SHIPS AND DATING

I don´t understand why and who you are dating

Or is this just again

A reflection of yourself

Your standards

Your will to grow – (with your partner)

I thought we are more similar to each other

Why are you looking for younger

Dumber

More feminine

Lower degree

Lower character

Than yourself

Why are you looking for someone you are already superior to?

Don´t you wanna grow?

Get motivated?

Get inspired by?

To dating like my generation

I really don´t understand the sense in your way of dating

I don´t see the point in meeting strangers

Dating strangers

Not knowing if you even like them

You don´t get to know somebody in like three dates

Maybe my trust is broken

But what is this shit?

With - I will wait till he or she loves me enough

So I can show her/him the way I really am

Because then they won´t leave me?

What the fuck

How self destructing can it get?

How low is your self esteem?

And how high is our self hate?

How can you play with your partners emotions?

When you don´t know what you are feeling for that person?

Why are you showing them so much affection?

Behaving like you already are in a relationship

But yeah we already have a name for this problem in our generation

It is called situation ships

Why are you getting caught up

Using so much on their energy on those toxic people

Who are you so dependent on their emotions?

Why are you are seeing people who are not willing to commit for you?

To stand up for you - Who are not showing you how much they value you

How much they respect you and your time and energy

How understanding they are if you cancel a date

How much they think about you and text you without any reason

How much they care for you as a person and not just your pussy

Who are not telling you how they are feeling for you

How much you mean to them

Who are not planning their future with you

And now I ask - why and how people (can) take this shit

People -who are loving and kind - maybe even naive

How can you let yourself be treated not the way you deserve to be treated

Of course I did go through this phase too

I loved affection

I fell for the guys who liked me

It was easier because there was no possible rejection

But I was 14 and dumb

How can you still do this "innocent" shit

Haven´t you learned a thing?

Why do you need a boyfriend so badly?

Can´t you be just happy by yourself?

Why is society telling us

We are only complete with a partner?

Why are sayings all like – you need to find your other half?

It implements you are not completed alone – you can´t be happy by yourself

But how about you people learn to love yourself first

You will see how lonely it gets

But also you will see how many beautiful people from the inside there are left

When you put yourself always first

Because you should never be their first priority

And your partner should never be your first priority

You should always be your own first priority

As should your partner be his/hers first as well

And I have been there

Lost myself

In pleasing my partner

Burning out while doing so

For what?

After the breakup

I felt as empty as before

While he was dating the next one

Replacing me

I used the pain and emptiness to gain strength to
learn to love myself

To fill the emptiness

by loving myself

And now I am afraid

To love another person again

Because I am afraid of loosing myself again

To find your true self

You have to get lost first

Maybe every time I will get lost in loving someone

I will learn something new

I will survive

I will come out stronger

NOBODY NEEDED

Thank your for hurting me again and again

So I can find to myself again

To show me

I can rely on myself again

Because I don´t need nobody

Nobody like you

SNOW WHITE

I now kissed my Snow White

It is awake now

Healing can begin now

Because I - my own prince started the process

I can begin to fall in love with the prince

I had become over the past few years

I had to become strong enough

To be able to heal myself

From my past

To heal my past self

Which was suppressed, abused, emotionally beaten up,
...

And I say never again

Now that I am falling in love with my own prince

With my hero

With my new self

I Scream **never again**

Will I let something like this happen again

To me

#iamnotvictim

#iamasurvivor

#iammyownhero

BROKEN GLASS

Trust

Lost so easily

Can trust be lost

By only one side

Destroyed by only one side?

Trust destroyed in thousand pieces

Who can I still trust when I am loosing my trust in
you

My friend

The one I live with

The one I share my life the most with

The one I share my flat – my home with

You who should know how long it took me to trust you

And you are playing with my trust

With every little inconsistency

With every little lie

With every little "not telling" me stuff

You cut me out of your life

you cut – cut – cut – cut out

a little piece of my trust for you

you keep cutting

You do this

I am just watching

Wondering

Crying

How you could treat me like this

Knowing all this about me

With my trust issues

And you still behaving like a little stupid kid

I just wanna kick you out of the room

I know its just your coping method

Because you are so little developed

You have not grown out of your past

But I am halfway trough my own shitty past – growing everyday

And your are still coping – denying - lying

You are beating everybody in the face

Who tries to help you

Like a little kid

You beat around yourself

Don´t care about the harm you take with your actions on others

Or who you beat up

Even if it is the person reaching out to you with their hand

Trying to help and support you

While you are lying on the ground

Beating everything coming near you

I think the only reason I keep letting you mistreat me like this

Is because I know

I am not the reason or fault in this situation

I am not to blame for your actions

You actions are only a way to express

How deeply you are still hurt, still damaged by your past

And how little time you invested in your own healing process

And bitterly I am strong enough to take all this shit

Hoping you can do better one day

Will do better one day

Because you decide to change

Out of your free will

I am here to tell you

I don´t care

How hurt you are

It is not and never will be an excuse to hurt other people - who did not harm you

And if you disagree - you are no better than the people who hurt you in the past - like your Parents did

Do you wanna be like your parents?

Or do you wanna become better?

Become a better or the best version of yourself?

I know - deep down

I am not the cause for your reaction

Because I see your little misbehaved kid in you

That is the reason I stay

Or maybe because I let you trigger me

Let you misbehave

Let you mistreat me

To learn for myself

To set boundaries

The hard way

Even with people I love

Especially on those people I have to learn this

Because Love should always mean acceptance

But trust and love also mean

That I can see you get hurt by your parents again

But also respecting what I am feeling at this moment

Because every time you are ignoring my warnings

How dangerous it is to trust the people who have hurt you so many times in the past

And you come to me hurt and crying

I can only tell you over and over again to stop seeing them

And instead of listening and understanding

You start not telling me – which for me is the same as lying – as you know – because I told you way too often

Because you know what I will reply

So you don´t tell me anymore

Because you don´t like what I have to say

And by this action

You keep cutting me out of your life

You keep deconstructing the trust

My trust for you

And because I have gone through this

I know how long and awful this journey is and will stay for a long time

To cut your parents out of your life

I am not completely there yet myself

So who am I to judge?

But the difference

I keep you in my life

I keep telling you everything about my life

Even if I know you won´t like it

And of course by doing so

What should I expect or think

When your parents come to visit you

When we agreed they should not even know our address

What am I suppose to think

With all this trust cut away

Of course my first thought will be that you did tell them by yourself

You were inconsistent again

And because you know about our agreement and my anger about it

That you break the trust again

You would not tell me – because it´ll be easier

As you did not do

Case closed?

I am so proud of myself in this situation

That although you sat on the floor crying

after your parents spontaneously visited us and you did not let them inside our apartment

I told you my thoughts about – what my first thought about not trusting you was

I am not proud of mistrusting you there

But this only shows – how much trust is left

And you told our address to your sister – who is still living with your parents

Yes we agreed on – it is okay she can visit us

But for me there is difference between visiting

And you telling her our address without her visiting out apartment yet

And of course without telling me this detail

That she knows it

Why are you keeping things from me?

Now I feel toxic

Because I am not worthy of information?

But I am proud because I felt my emotions

And I told you about it

And because I have gone through this

I know how long and awful this journey is and will stay for a long time

STABILITY

Maybe I have to give stability to myself

Because that is the first thing coming to my mind

I am looking for

I am seeking badly

Because it is missing

I am sick of all these changes

Changes in who I cannot trust if they are good or bad

Yeah I know I am and I have a butterfly mind

But sometimes a little more stability and the feeling of being grounded feels missing

Security - just feeling safe and home

Even in my own body I feel lost - too often

Because I do too much or too many things at the same time - taking too much of myself

I seek stability in a partner

Someone who was through a lot

Someone who can hold me in my tornado times

When everything seems to be flying out of my hands -
Out of my control

I want somebody who I can fall into their arms

In my worst times and someone who can hold me

Someone who is grounded - who is rooted enough

Someone I won´t drown with me

Someone who can carry my weight/burden - with me -
together

Help me carry it - until I can carry it by myself

How about I work on giving this to myself

Give myself a pause - to work on me

To get stronger

To carry this weight

Or maybe to get smarter

To work smarter - not harder

To unpack my carriage first

And then lift it

To carry it completely with success on my own

Because I became rooted in myself

So every tornado in my mind

Would have no harm anymore

Because I became rooted in loving myself

SO DONE

I am so done explaining myself

PEOPLE PLEASING

I am what I think you think I am

NEW FRIENDS

Isn´t it funny how you get new friends out of old or bad or ending friendships

Because you befriend a person you get to know their inner circle

Their friends

Sometimes the first friendship ends

But you gained one or two friends through this old friend of yours

You won new friends through

You gained a better friend than before

With every ending

So don´t fear the end

Because there will always follow a new beginning

Maybe even force the end

For a fresh start

For a better future

Maybe even with the same person

There could be a new beginning in the future

When both parts must go through some shit

Alone

Maybe there is hope

For a future together

With more understanding the other side

FUTURE IMPLODING

I am not crying because what happened

I am crying because every piece of a future of us together breaks into a thousand pieces

Because of the present time

Because what you are saying vs. what you are doing

I know

I see

That you are hurt – though you don't tell me – though you said – no – you promised you would

I keep telling you

You hurt me with this

With that

That I am deeply worried about my trust left for you

You remaining still

Saying nothing

I am telling you what actions hurt me – and you keep hurting me

I am telling you that I am questioning your personality and that I hope you don't do it on purpose

Though I am questioning it and keep it as a possibility

Because I told you how to trigger me

I told you how to hurt me

And I keep telling you with what actions you keep hurting me

And you keep hurting me by doing exact these things to me

Are doing this – hurting me – to self sabotage yourself?

To push – again– the person that is too close to you

That knows you too good

To push that exact person away?

By hurting that person

You keep losing all your friends

Because you keep pushing them away

By acting like an egoistic, idiotic little child

Hurting everybody around you

By replacing them with strangers

I come to the conclusion that

I think that your behavior says more about you and your character

Than it does – when it comes to my actions and my character

DROWNING WEIGHT

I know now why I have this feeling I can´t breathe
properly anymore

A heavy thing is resting on my chest - keeping me
from breathing

Pressing the air out of my lungs

I know now what it is

This heavy object

It is the weight of my package

Package full of my past, my traumas

My package that I left alone

That I loaded more and more by ignoring it

Even self sabotaging myself

By carrying the package with somebody else

So I only carried 50% of it

Now the other person who is gone

Reloading the full weight back on me

It feels like the weight is drowning me

Now it is time again to measure the trauma, the past, the weight of my package

It is time again to unpack things

To let go of the past

So I can carry this weight alone by myself

Without having the urge to sharing carrying my package

Now I have to enable myself again to carry my own past alone again

To rewrite my past

So I won´t need anybody to help me carry

I will never ever again put my weight on somebody else's shoulders

So if the person leaving – again – no matter the reason

It won´t fall back on me

It won´t break my rips

It won´t take my breath away – not again

I have learned this lesson

Because I am able to carry my life and my problems packed up in this package alone by myself

If somebody is sharing the weight of your package

It is simpler to not let your past affect you

I can breath now again – because I have a plan

Because now it is the time to put my package down

Let it stand on the ground

To unpack it – to put everything that was still resting on my shoulders out of this box

I will sort things out

This will take time

But it will be time where I get to know myself better

Where I and only I have the power to let my past go

This feeling of not being able to breathe will pass too

This feeling shall pass – like my past

My thought of the day

#Valentinesdaythoughts

EMPTY WORDS

I don´t even feel stuck anymore between emotions

First I felt replaced

Not good enough

Not worth of being loved

Replaceable

Being hurt by the fact you were already replaced

By someone not even similar to you

It is more about the words

The words your friend told you all over again

Like a prayer

"I could never replace you - Because you are irreplaceable"

That I have so much worth to their life - your friend promised to never replace you

And still they did replace you

That hurts

Because first you have to learn

Their worthlessness of their words

how meaningless and empty their words really are

hearing them

all those lies

and then there is this feeling of being happy

getting bigger the more information I am learning

by getting to know your real YOU

happy that my eyes were opened

aggressively opened – which hurt

but they are open now

I can see her now the way she truly is

The one with many faces

She shows to the world

Which is sad

But mostly for her

I wouldn't say I lost a lot of time with her

I learned so much – and I am still learning

While being hurt by her

While I let it happen – she keeps hurting me

By her words and not taking actions

Even though she promised she would take action from now on

Promises she won't hurt me anymore while I was sobbing in pain explaining to her why and how she did hurt me – what I wish for the better future

Trust broken

Everything

And still I don´t know what to feel

Even though now I should know how toxic she is

How she is betraying people

Friends

Not only me

Lies leaving her lips so effortlessly

She is cheating on people

While she keeps telling everyone in her life she loves them

They have no clue – who she is and what she does

She is fucking crazy

She is fucking toxic

I don´t feel replaced anymore

I don´t even want to change positions with the person I got replaced with

Maybe even rescued by that person – which is that position I was a long time

Without knowing her faces

I don´t mind getting replaced

Cause now I am free of a toxic person

She chose somebody else she can damage now

She can have power over

I am free now

I am free

Maybe she knows now that I am strong enough to cut
her out of my life

That I don´t really need her in my life

So she cut me out

She tries to cut me out by trying to replace me with
some version is nearly anything like me

But also somebody who is naive

Who wants to see the best in people

Someone who has trauma in her past

Talking to her ex lover has helped both of us

Because now we caught her

We caught her cheating on her ex lover with so many
people

Besides the fact she fucked those peoples, had
relationships with people - while having the
relationship with that girl not living nearby (I did
not even know about her existence)- who she was
cheating on - she told me she is in love with me and
those other relationships ended because those other
partners cheated on her

She told me so often - she is deeply in love with me

And I always replied that I am not and never will be

Her love for me was a burden for our friendship

It always let me question the real reason for our
friendship

Does she want more? Does she want a romantic relationship with me?

I am just happy to be replaced

I don´t want to change positions

It is quite simple

I am very happy now

That my eyes were opened

That I can see clear now

Who she is and what she has done

To me

But also to other friends/lovers

It gets easier

Because I am not the only one who got caught up on her potential

What do we three women have in common?

The three women she loves

The three women she claims to love

We have traumatic pasts

2 out of 3 have traumas with men – the third I don´t know well enough

We saw the worst in people

In men especially

Because of that we want to see the good in people

We are naive

We want to trust people

We tend to ignore red flags

Maybe this is our weak spot

Our blind spot

We are too good to see the bad in people

We don´t see the bad in people anymore

We are naive

We want to have connections, bonding with people we trust

We seek trust

Toxic

She cheated on her girlfriend with other bitches – while telling me she loves me and her "relationships" she used for cheating on her girlfriend – I did know of – telling me those bitches cheated on her – WTF

Now her ex lover knows she betrayed her

STILL CRYING

Why am I crying

Now?

Now that I am free and by myself

Free of the people that I felt prisoned by

Free of the people that I felt held back by

Mistreated by

I now find things that remember me

Of the good times

And what trust I put in them - back then

I had one of them in my fucking last will

We had so many plans and dreams to accomplish together

Maybe I am just crying over this potential future never coming true

We planned to move out of my apartment together

Splitting all the costs

Me being responsible - again

Me breaking the bond to my parents - with them in my back to secure me

Me lending them money, having the greatest risk of us all

But all were worth it

Were they?

Now I am just happy this apartment plans never became reality

Now I know my bad feeling about all this responsibility became reality

Because the trust was and still is broken

Not fixable

I am crying because who can I trust now?

Can I even trust myself after this?

Because I lost perspective so hardly?

I saw more potential in them –

I was willing to sacrifice so much for their potential

Why am I giving myself up so easily for others

But when it comes to helping myself – seeing potential in myself

Working on myself as I work on others

Being nice to myself and not as critical as to others

I should really learn this

WHO AM I?

WHO Am I - based on my pictures I have on my phone

Who am I based on my pictures on Instagram - what is my appearance on others? How do they see me - what do they see in me?

EMPATHS

Can you bee too empathic?

Too sensitive?

Because I am feeling too much

I feel everything

I am feeling what another person is feeling

Even if it is fake

Like on tv

They cry - I cry

They are happy - I am happy

I am like a sponge

Sucking everything in

GRIEVING

Maybe it is not always talking

It is just sitting with the other person

Grieving in silence

Facing the pain in silence

Supporting each other in silence

PAIN

Pain makes life livable

Pain reminds me I am still breathing

I am still alive

RUN AWAY

I just wanna dive into another reality

Feel somebody else's emotions

Rather than my own

SUPPORT BY OTHERS

I ask myself is it less scary?

It is less scary – doing something that scares the shit out of you

If you have someone by your side

You can trust your life with?

You can fully rely on – lean on?

(Not just people you are connected to you by genetics – Who feel responsible to be there)

DECISIONS

What am I afraid of?

living?

dying?

How about I live first.

And stop being afraid of life.

MY BODY - MY MIND - MY PAIN

I am self sabotaging again

What if I seek a body which represents how broken I am

Or more likely how broken I feel inside?

With me working on my mental health

Doing the inner work

Finally

I will also heal my muscle soreness, my high muscle tension...

How tight my body is

How weak my body is

How fragile

I will workout

I do the inner and outta work

I will be strong -> inside out

My joints - holding my body together

My body seems to be strong - from far away

I can lift heavy things but pain will follow me

My joints aren't mobile

Aren't flexible enough

I have to work on my joints - holding my body together

While everything feeling like it is falling apart

But I have to strengthen my joints

I'll show people how to treat me

By showing them how I treat myself

I will now give myself the care I have always
deserved and asked for

I will love myself unconditionally

I will show others how to do so

RE-BUILDING

my head is spinning

my thoughts are racing

my mind is a mess

a mess full of pieces

I have to rebuild my mind - my mind castle

brick by brick

stone by stone

this time it will stand out every rain shower

every thunderstorm

every earthquake

I have learned my lesson

I now take the old pieces which remind me of all my
failures

I´ll burn everything down

So I can mix every old decision I made with the ones
I am making now

Every good and bad decision mixed together will
become the new bricks which will build my foundation
for my castle

The first bricks are the hardest

And even if some parts will fall apart
- again -
Remember it is a process

Not everything will fall apart
So I can redecorate my castle
Add rooms
Maybe even secret rooms
Or guest rooms
I am the architect
I can decide

Even though I can´t see clear through all the smoke
at the moment
Because everything is burning
I will remember this one
From the ashes we will rise

→ The castle symbols your character traits

RE-LIVING

What if I can only feel my emotions through (re)living it with other persons while they are feeling those emotions?

REALITY

It can be without knowing it is true

CHANGE OF WORDS

What if I call everything different?

It is not sex anymore

It is now naked time or whatever

Maybe it will be easier doing it then

When there is no negative past memories to that word

Drowning me down

Stopping it from experimenting

Stopping me from exploring new things

This time positively

ALL THE THINGS I FELT WITH HER

I felt seen

I felt close

I felt less alone

I felt understood

Now I lost all of it

And I am grieving

It feels like I've lost somebody I cared about

Cared about more than I care about myself

I feel like I lost a sister

I feel like I am leftover

Now I have nothing left to loose

Only myself

You have to get lost first

Before you can find your true self right?

THE PERSON I WAS AROUND HER IS DEAD

The Person I am around her

The Person I could have become around her

DIED

I learned so much about myself

by being around a friend

But Friendships can end

so my version of being around this friend died with this friendship

and this shit hurts

#frienshipsmindhurtful

EMOTIONS

I am feeling taken for granted

I never want to feel like that again

HOPE

I actually don´t hope for it

But

I kind a hope

It is the solution

My solution

That the things I feel the urge to do

Writing the truth

Writing about my past

To heal myself

Will be my solution to it all

WHAT ABOUT THAT THOUGHT

You just try always your fucking best

Always

No matter what

Only then you know you did everything you could

Just do 10% more than you think you could do

You won´t have any regrets

With the knowledge you have done everything in your power

A life without regrets – sounds great

GIVE 100%

Not playing safe

Taking risks

Play hard, play smart

But do everything in your power

e.g. to keep somebody

ABOUT LOVE

The next time you really like someone

Just tell them

What do you have to loose?

Just try it

If it is not how something supposed to be

How imagined it

Open your god damn mouth and tell it

Spit it out

NEW LIFE MOTTO

Try everything

work hard and smart

Give 100%

And if it is not for you

It is not meant for you

And just tell the fucking truth

Your truth - always without exceptions

NO WORDS LEFT FOR A LOST FRIEND

You did everything in your power

You have no regret

Because you told her everything

You told her everything you wanted to say

Until the point you had no more words left to say

You did come to the point you had no more words left
to be wasted on her deaf ears

No words would changed a thing

SYMPTOMS

I never experienced violence

against my body

At least in a physical harming way

But the things I had to do with my body

That is a whole different story

on the emotional and psychological level

there was violence

there was abuse

messing with my own head

by family members

but by the states it is no crime

only when there is physical violence

now I don't know if I should be thankful

but also

now I wonder

I am sitting here

Wondering if my symptoms existed from the beginning
or were triggered by this "violence"

Did I developed these symptoms

Of borderline, ADHD etc.?

FEELING LIKE A MAN

Sometimes I am feeling like a man

I am trying to prove myself

To the world and to prove my self worth

I want to prove I am smart and everything

Even with all my accomplishments I already have

I am still not happy about it

And I don´t know why

I feel like a man

I feel like I had to become my own father

I had become the man who had never nurtured me

Who had never educated me

Who was never a role model

I just realized I had become the person

Who hasn´t had any time for me

My dad

Because I wanted to know what my dad had that was
worthier than me

That was making him want to spend his time with his
thing

instead of spending his time with me

it is like

kids who have drug addicts as parents become addicts
themselves

because they simply want to know that pleasure

that dopamine kick

which is more worthy than their kids

with my dad

his drug is work

he is a workaholic

now I became that kind of woman who duplicates her
father

because he was never there

they way I needed him to be

on an emotional loving level

I am not kind a trying to be like the man I want to
marry

I am becoming the duplicate of my father

That is a harsh truth I guess

BEING WOMAN

Don't hold my ponytail

Hold my hips instead

I don't need long hair you can Grab

Take a Look at my hips

They will do the job

SHE LEFT

How fucking crazy is this. The narcissist found an easier victim than me.

She found someone who believed her lies faster and easier than I did

She left

Because the other one was easier to manipulate

She left

Because I saw potential in her

Which made me criticize her

Which she could not handle

No matter how soft my words were

How wisely I chose those words

WHAT A COMPLIMENT OF A NARCISSIST

To be left

Because it was too hard to manipulate me

Because I am no good victim

I´m too strong

To be left

Because a new victim was weaker

Like the lion stopped hunting the black panther

Because deep down the lion knew

He would loose the race against the panther

The lion is slower and weaker

I WANT TO BREAK FREE

Why do I put myself in a cage?

Good question

Better question

Why does it feel safer to be in a cage than to be outside and free

How can something I dreamed of my entire life

Scares me so much

Freedom

How can I feel more at home in a cage than to be free

Because I always was in a cage and it felt like home.

It is home. It became home.

My life lived in a cage.

So it is more comfortable to stay there.

I wan to break free

LOST AT SEA

What trauma and coping feels like

I feel lost

At sea

In a boat

Alone

Nothing is worse

But when the sea is still

Still no is land in sight

That is the most terrifying moment

When you are in a thunderstorm

You don´t think

You are busy surviving

There is no endless mind suffering

No ending thoughts

Just surviving

Healing is seeing land

You are willing to paddle to this destination

No matter how long it will take

You have a goal in sight

It is a long process

You are strong

The moment you have reached the land

The harbor

You are looking for an anchor

To secure your boat

To secure your body

It is in need of an anchor

You are afraid to feel secure again

Of course for someone who has been lost at sea for years

You are not afraid of the land

It is just a strange feeling to feel secure again

At first you don´t even know what to feel the first time you touch the land

Should you feel safe

Are you safe now?

Is it just an illusion?

Not running away - Back to your boat

Just to get that usual feeling of up and down back

It is the chaos you know – from early on

I think peace is something to learn

And chaos to unlearn

You have to learn to love the peace

You have to learn to love the patience to wait

You have to learn to love the fear of boredom

Boredom is to accept on this journey

MINIMALISTIC

Another thing I am changing my mind about

My parents are materialistic

I think I am a minimalist

I don´t need much

I look at all the stuff I own

Feeling all the pressure

I don´t want to keep any of it

I only want to move out with things I need daily

Everything I own is rebuy able

FREEDOM

I realize now the difference between

Emotional bonding and material wealth

I thought I have an emotional attachment to so many objects

but

Everything is forgettable

Like all my coffee mugs

Would I miss all of them

Or only one

Or none?

You can rebuy everything there is

I think you won´t miss a thing

If you left everything behind

A hard truth

But also freeing at the same time

The truth frees you

Even the expensive sunglasses

Bought for the vacation in Australia

Not even by my own money

Still I own it

It collects dust on my shelf

It wasn´t worn since this vacation in 2014

The moment I don´t have a use for it

It goes away

I was raised different

That is why it is hard at the beginning

But it is getting easier

MURDER OF YOUR PARENTS

A strange feeling to have as a young adult

You have killed your parents

Your parents are dead

The truth

You just killed the idea

The wish

The hope

Of your child inside you

Your parents are never going to be the ones you need

What you always wished them to be

As a child

A loving

Caring

Emotionally available parents

I am not saying you will never have people like this
in your life

I am just saying they will never be like this

That is not your fault

That is actually their pity

There is so much to love in this world

Now you killed that idea

You killed your parents

You killed the emotional detachment you felt towards them

But in truth you broke that bond along time ago

You are just realizing this right now

They are already dead to you

Fact

That is why

On a funeral of someone else, the thought of yourself burying your parents

Did not let you feel a thing

You felt horrible about that

Normally you should feel something

A lot of something

Now you are standing there

With tears in your eyes

Because you cannot feel a thing

Even with the imagination of your both parents dead

Because you buried them along time ago

And that shit hurts

Because it is not meant to be this way

That makes me cry

In my head they are already dead to me

they are still alive and this does not make it easier

On an emotional level they stay dead

They were never actually there

This is a hard truth

I am crying for the loss

I accept the loss

I am grieving for the people I never had in my life

For the mother that I always wished for

I am grieving for my dad I always wished for but never had

This is a hard truth

The fact they are still alive makes it even worst

If they are still alive there is a little hope left

That I can change them

I cannot change them

I can only live this grieve

Accept this and my life will start

I can take a look at my past, work on my traumas, work on appreciating what a great person I become through all the odds

What I did to become this person

Worship this

Give myself credit for this – for my past

I somehow raised myself

I was my own mother, my own dad, my own sister

My own family

Sometimes I felt so lonely

But the next moment I didn´t felt lonely

Because I had to become all those roles

It is so sad

That even back then I had to raise my parents as well

When they fought

I was the one – debating with everyone of them alone

Arrange they will make compromises

I had to become the adult

I had too many roles growing up

I had to mature too early

Now I am sitting here

Typing this

Crying

Feeling like a little child again

Not knowing where to start working

Not knowing anything at all will work

I hate that feeling of feeling broken

the uncertainty where to start to glue me back together

the pieces lying on the floor

all this potential – my potential

Gluing myself together became a hobby

I did it so often – I stopped counting

Building a new figure

A new me

And still there are parts of me I did not use

Because they did not fit into the new figure I was creating

Glued back together – by me

That should have been stronger

All the time I am breaking – sometimes I am breaking myself through self sabotaging habits I picked up

Destructing my own piece of art into pieces again

now I want to show I learned my lessons

So I can glue myself together the way I won´t break anymore

Or at least only one piece will fall of and not the whole figure I was building

Printed in Great Britain
by Amazon

24077999R00056